anythink

D0884676

It's an Orca!

by Mari Schuh

LERNER PUBLICATIONS ◆ MINNEAPOLIS

Note to Educators:

Throughout this book, you'll find critical thinking questions. These can be used to engage young readers in thinking critically about the topic and in using the text and photos to do so.

For Natalie —MS

Lerner Publications Company
A division of Lerner Publishing Group, Inc.
241 First Avenue North
Minneapolis, MN 55401 USA

For reading levels and more information, look up this title at www.lernerbooks.com.

Library of Congress Cataloging-in-Publication Data

Names: Schuh, Mari C., 1975– author.
Title: It's an orca! / Mari Schuh.
Other titles: It is an orca!
Description: Minneapolis : Lerner Publications, [2019] | Series: Bumba books. Polar animals | Audience: Ages 4–7. | Audience: K to grade 3. | Includes bibliographical references and index.
Identifiers: LCCN 2018000931 (print) | LCCN 2017057032 (ebook) | ISBN 9781512482867 (eb pdf) | ISBN 9781512482805 (lb : alk. paper) | ISBN 9781541526983 (pb : alk. paper)
Subjects: LCSH: Killer whale—Juvenile literature.
Classification: LCC QL737.C432 (print) | LCC QL737.C432 S42875 2019 (ebook) | DDC 599.53/6—dc23

LC record available at https://lccn.loc.gov/2018000931

Manufactured in the United States of America
1-43313-33133-5/1/2018

Table of Contents

Orcas Swim

Orcas are huge ocean animals.

They are black and white.

Orcas are a kind of dolphin.

Can you think of other animals that are black and white?

Orcas swim in

every ocean.

They often swim in

cold water.

Orcas are fast.

Wide tails help them swim.

Flippers help them turn.

Why would it be helpful for orcas to be fast swimmers?

Orcas have a thick layer of fat.

The fat is called blubber.

Blubber keeps them warm in

the cold water.

Often orcas are called
killer whales.
Orcas got that name
because they eat whales.

Orcas are hunters.

Some orcas hunt in groups called pods.

Other orcas hunt alone.

Why might orcas hunt in groups?

Orcas hunt fish and squid.

They also hunt sharks and seals.

Some orcas slide out
of the water.
They grab penguins
on the ice.

Orcas do not chew their food.

They swallow it whole.

Or they tear it into small pieces.

Parts of an Orca

Picture Glossary

blubber

fat on orcas and other ocean animals

flippers

flat body parts that stick out from an orca's side

pods

groups of orcas that swim together

squid

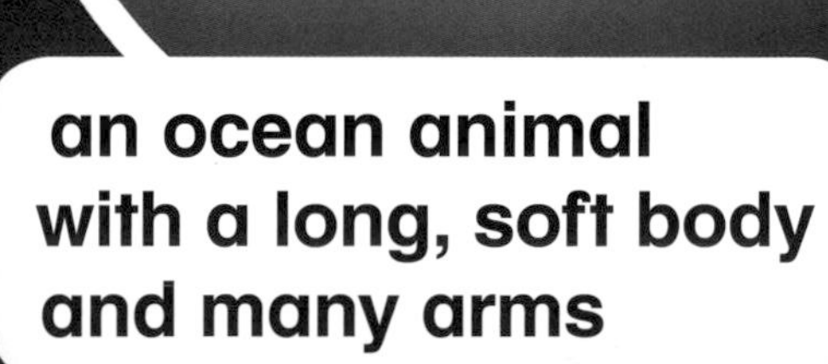

an ocean animal with a long, soft body and many arms

Read More

Adamson, Heather. *Orcas.* Minneapolis: Bellwether Media, 2018.

Riggs, Kate. *Killer Whales.* Mankato, MN: Creative Education/Creative Paperbacks, 2017.

Schuh, Mari. *It's a Narwhal!* Minneapolis: Lerner Publications, 2019.

Index

Photo Credits

Image credits: icons: Amy Salveson/Independent Picture Service; Calvin Hall/First Light/Getty Images, p. 5; wildestanimal/Moment/Getty Images, pp. 7, 23 (bottom left); Rolf Hicker/All Canada Photos/Getty Images, p. 8; Thomas Kitchin & Victoria Hurst/All Canada Photos/Getty Images, p. 10; Doug Perrine/Photolibrary/Getty Images, p. 13; Ron Sanford/Corbis Documentary/Getty Images, p. 14; vladsilver/Shutterstock.com, p. 16; Mark Carwardine/ Minden Pictures/Getty Images, p. 21; bennymarty/iStock/Getty Images, p. 22; Danita Delimont/ Gallo Images/Getty Images, p. 23 (top left); Chase Dekker Wild-Life Images/Moment/Getty Images, p. 23 (top right); Jeff Rotman/Photolibrary/Getty Images, p. 23 (bottom right).

Cover: Christopher Meder/Shutterstock.com.